INDIAN CONSTITUTION *for* CHILDREN

Smt. Rajendra Kumari
District & Sessions Judge (retired),
Bihar

Dr. S. S. Awasthy
Associate Professor (retired), Political Science,
Delhi University

Publishers
UNICORN BOOKS
F-2/16, Ansari Road, Daryaganj, New Delhi-110002
☎ Ph.: 011-23262683, 23250704, 45644782
E-mail: info@unicornbooks.in • *Website:* www.unicornbooks.in

ISBN 978-81-7806-578-6

Edition: 2024

Printed at : Param Offsetters, Okhla, New Delhi-110020

Preface

The Constitution of India is a fundamental document which defines the power and functions of the three organs of the government at the level of the Union as well as the States. It has proved to be the greatest national inspirational force, the new slogans of *Sabka Saath, Sabka Vikas* and 'less Government, more Governance', are ideal objectives. It also provides for various fundamental and legal rights to the citizens.

The Constitution contains Preamble, Directive Principles of State Policy, and fundamental Duties which proclaim the basic values and together they constitute the Fundamental Principles of the Constitution. This Constitution was implemented successfully and has delivered positive goods to the different sections of the society.

The study of the Constitution demands a high degree of accuracy for which a small attempt has been made.

Rajendra Kumari
Dr. S.S. Awasthy

Contents

INDIAN CONSTITUTION FOR CHILDREN

1

INTRODUCTION

What makes India of today different from what it was many centuries ago? After nearly 200 years of British rule, India got freedom on 15th August 1947. Today, we are a free people. Ours is a democratic country, in which people decide as to who will govern them. All sovereign powers vest in 'We, the people'.

People do this by electing their representatives who are elected for a specific period, say 5 years, after which elections are again conducted to elect their representatives. This way the process goes on for ever. This is in contrast to old days when we used to have kings and queens who ruled us just because they belonged to the Royal Family. But now we rule ourselves, as citizens of the country and we are very much a part of the government which exists today.

The phrase 'of the people, by the people, for the people' was first used by US President Abraham Lincoln on 19 November 1863, during his famous speech at Gettysburg.

The entire structure of the government and the various principles that bind the institution of government have their origin in the constitution of India. It is the sheet-anchor of our democracy. It set some limits on what a government can impose on its citizens; these limits are fundamental that government may never trespass them. Constitution tells us what the fundamental nature of our society is.

A constitution helps serve as a set of rules and principles

that all persons in the country can agree upon as the basis of the way in which they want the country to be governed. This includes the type of government and also an agreement on certain ideals that they believe the country should uphold. The second important purpose of a constitution is to define the nature of country's political system.

The very first fundamental duty of every citizen of India should be to abide by the constitution and respect its ideals and institutions. To be able to do so, we need to know our constitution, understand how we are governed and to what extent the ideals set by the founding fathers are being fulfilled.

Our constitution was created in the aftermath of a popular, national movement. It drew upon a long history of nationalist movement. It is a written document, which lays down the procedure and rules of governance so that all the people of the country live together peacefully. As there are rules for the games like football, hockey or cricket and we call them the governing rules of the game, likewise society also has certain governing rules that makes it what it is. These governing rules are in a written document which is called constitution. All democratic countries have a constitution.

■■■

2

FUNCTIONS OF A CONSTITUTION

A constitution is a basic law of the country and it performs many functions in the society. The first function of a constitution is to provide basic rules of governance to the society. The second equally important function of the constitution is to decide as to what kind of government it will be and how it will be constituted. While doing so it sets some limit on the powers of the government. Another important function of the constitution is to divide power between the various organs of the state, i.e. legislature, executive and judiciary so that there is no confusion and everybody works in a systematic way. It also contains certain ideals which the country must uphold.

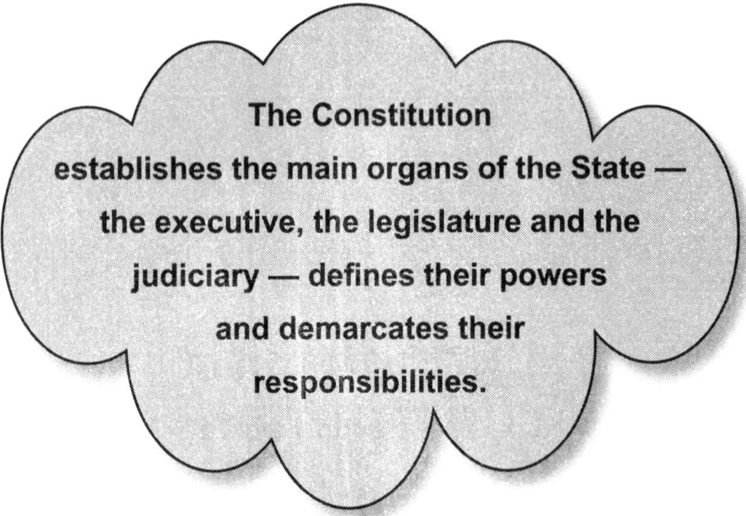

The constitution also provides for the basic liberties and freedoms for the members of the society which the government must respect and never trespass them. In fact, a constitution is known by the freedom it provides. This is also called 'bill of rights.'

Many countries have two sets of government. This is called federal form of government and in such a system of government the constitution divides the powers between the central government and state governments. At both levels, governments have to work within the limits set by the constitution.

The Constitution is enacted for a long time. The oldest constitution is the US Constitution which was made in 1789 and it is continuing to exist. But this does not mean that the constitution is static. Nothing in this world is static and so is the constitution. The Constitution is a living document, and it should be revised with the changing needs and aspirations of the members of society. For example, the US Constitution has been amended 33 times to add new changes. For this purpose, every constitution provides a procedure for changing or amending it. Indian constitution has also been changed over the years to reflect new concerns of the polity. However, the basics and fundamental principles have remained unchanged.

■■■

3

MAKING OF THE INDIAN CONSTITUTION

As you know, we became free on 15 August 1947. This freedom was achieved after a long struggle against the British rule. Almost in the end of freedom struggle in 1946, a Constituent Assembly was constituted which 'drafted' the Indian Constitution. The work on the making of constitution was started on December 9, 1946 and it was finally approved by the members of the Constituent Assembly on November 26, 1949. The Constituent Assembly took nearly three years to prepare it. The original version of the Indian constitution was handwritten in English, in exquisite calligraphy by Prem

Behari Narain Raizada, and the calligraphy of the Hindi version was done by Vasant Krishan Vaidya, and each page was decorated with beautiful illustrations by a team of artists led by the famous painter from Santiniketan, Nandlal Bose. Part III on Fundamental Rights carries an illustration of Ram, Sita and Lakshman, when they were returning Ayodhya.

On January 24, 1950, 284 members of the Constituent Assembly signed both the English as well as the Hindi version of the Constitution. It was also the day when our national anthem *jangan man adhinayak jai he*, written by poet Rabindra Nath Tagore, was adopted by the Constituent Assembly.

The Constitution of India was drafted by the people who enjoyed immense public credibility, had the capacity to negotiate and command the respect of wide-cross spectrum of the society. Most of them were actively involved in the freedom struggle, and in the process of freedom struggle, they had understood the problems and aspirations of the masses. The final document reflected the broad national consensus at that time.

Under the British rule, the Indians were forced to obey rules that were not made by them. The long experience of authoritarian rule convinced Indians that free India should be a democracy in which a democratic government would be set up, and the prescribed rules would determine its functioning.

This was done not by one person but by a group of around 300 people who became members of the Constituent Assembly in 1946 and met periodically for next three years to write India's constitution. It was a very challenging job but the members of the Constituent Assembly rose to the occasion and gave this country a visionary document that reflected respect for diversity while preserving national unity. In fact, the Constituent Assembly had a galaxy of scholars, lawyers and leaders. The most prominent among them were Jawahar Lal Nehru, Sarojini Naidu, K.M.Munshi, Maulana Azad, Sardar Patel, Dr. B.R.Ambedkar, Shyama Prasad Mukerjee, Govind Ballabh Pant, Jagjivan Ram, Baldev Singh, Purushottam Das Tandon and Dr. Rajendra Prasad who was also elected as the President of the Constituent Assembly.

The proceedings of the Constituent Assembly from 1946 to 1949 have been printed in twelve thick volumes called Constituent Assembly Debates. It shows how carefully everything was discussed and deliberated upon.

In order to make a constitution for free India, the constitutions of about 60 countries such as U.S.A., France, Ireland etc. were studied and many good features from these constitutions were borrowed and included in the Indian Constitution. The Government of India Act, 1935 was also studied, and to a great extent our constitution is influenced by this Government of India Act 1935 which was passed by the British Parliament during the colonial period. In fact, the makers of the Indian Constitution did not start with a clean slate. During the British rule, as a result of freedom movement, many constitutional reforms took place and the makers of the constitution took them as foundations and developed them further.

On August 29, 1947, a Drafting Committee having eight members was formed under the chairmanship of Dr. B. R. Ambedkar to prepare a draft of the constitution on the basis of the decisions taken by the Constituent Assembly. The Drafting Committee submitted its draft on February

21, 1948, and further debates were held and on the basis of these debates a new draft was prepared and submitted to the Assembly on November 4, 1948.

This draft was then discussed in the country and further debated in the Constituent Assembly and ultimately on November 26, 1949, the constitution was given the final shape. Our Constitution in its original form had 395 Articles and 8 Schedules.

On completion of this monumental work, the Chairman of the Drafting Committee, Dr Ambedkar said, **'The Constitution can provide only the Organs of State such as the Legislature, the Executive and the Judiciary. The factors on which the working of these organs depends are the people and the political parties they will set up as their instruments to carry out their wishes and their politics. Who can say how the people of India and their parties will behave?'**

Dr Rajendra Prasad, the President of the Constituent assembly in his concluding speech sounded words of caution and wisdom. He observed, **'If the people who are selected are capable, and of character and integrity, they would be able to make the best even of a defective Constitution. If they are lacking in these, the Constitution cannot help the country.'**

The Constitution became fully effective from January 26, 1950. It was also the day when India became republic with Dr. Rajendra Prasad as its first President. Since then, we celebrate January 26, 1950 as our Republic Day.

Salient Features of the Indian Constitution

1. **A Written Document:** Some constitutions are unwritten like the British Constitution. But the Indian Constitution is written on paper. As we learnt above, a constituent assembly was specifically created to make the Constitution for India.

2. **The Largest Constitution:** The Indian Constitution is the largest constitution in the world. It contains 22 Parts, 12 Schedules and 395 Articles. The reason of it being lengthy is that all the minute details dealing with the administrative and political system of the country have been included in the Constitution.

3. **Rigid and Flexible:** Usually a constitution is either rigid like the U.S. Constitution or flexible like the British Constitution. But the Indian Constitution is a blend of both. Many provisions can be changed or amended easily but the basic structure cannot be changed. Our constitution has been amended 105 times till August 2021.

4. **Federal:** Our Constitution is federal which means the powers have been clearly divided between the Union Government on the one hand and the State Governments on the other. This is necessary because India is a big country and it can not be governed from one place. At

both levels, the governments act on the areas allotted to them. But certainly, the Union Government has more powers than the State Governments.

5. **The Indian Constitution begins with a Preamble:** Every book has an introduction in which the author briefly gives a summary of the book. The author also gives reasons as to why he wrote the book. The preamble is similar to the introduction of any book. It summarises the objectives of writing the Indian Constitution. It summarises the ideals and aspirations of the Indian people as visualised by the framers of the Constitution. One of the ideals of the constitution was to transform Indian society; tackle all social and economic problems in due course and make India a successful democracy by removing socio-economic inequalities. Usually, all the constitutions in the world start with a preamble. But the form, contents and style of its presentation differ in all the constitutions. But the objective of having a preamble

is always the same. The Preamble generally sets the ideals and goals for the makers of the constitution what they desire to achieve through the constitution. The importance and utility of the preamble lives in the fact that it embodies the spirit or ideology of the constitution. It also aids the legal interpretation of the constitution when the language is found to be ambiguous. The Indian Constitution also contains a preamble which reflects the wishes and objectives of the makers of our Constitution.

■■■

4

THE PREAMBLE

The Preamble is a part of the Constitution and was enacted and adopted by the same procedure as the rest of the Constitution. One of the members of the Constituent Assembly commented very beautifully about the Preamble that, "The Preamble is the most precious part of the constitution. It is the soul of the Constitution. It is a key to the Constitution." Truly it has been hailed as a 'jewel' set in the Constitution. In fact, the Preamble contains all the essentials of the Indian Constitution.

The Preamble

WE, THE PEOPLE OF INDIA, having solemnly
resolved to constitute India into a
SOVEREIGN SOCIALIST
SECULAR DEMOCRATIC REPUBLIC
and to secure to all its citizens:
JUSTICE, social, economic and political;
LIBERTY of thought, expression, belief,
faith and worship;
EQUALITY of Status and of opportunity;
and to promote among them all
FRATERNITY assuring the dignity of the individual
and the
UNITY AND INTEGRITY OF THE NATION;
IN OUR CONSTITUENT ASSEMBLY
this twenty sixth day of November, 1949,
do HEREBY ADOPT, ENACT AND GIVE TO
OURSELVES THIS CONSTITUTION.

The Preamble contains the following attributes:

Sovereign

The Preamble declares India to be a sovereign country. It means absolute and supreme power not subject to control by any internal or external authority; and it is free to take its own decisions without interference from any other country or organisation. Another essential attribute as a value enshrined in the Constitution is that sovereignty vests in the people. It is 'We, the People' who are sovereign and who have given 'to ourselves this Constitution'. All the functionaries including the highest ones of the State are accountable to us (the People).

Socialist and Secular

The terms Socialist and Secular were included in the Indian Constitution by 42nd Constitutional Amendment Act in 1977. The term 'Socialist' means that the aim of the Constitution is elimination of inequality in income, status and standards of life; and to establish a society based on justice – social, economic and political. The term 'Secular' implies *Sarva dhram Sambhava* i.e. treating all religions alike and giving equal respect to all the religions. There is no official or state religion in India and people are free to practice and propagate any religion and faith.

Democratic

The term 'Democratic' postulates that the people are supreme and the government is created and exists at the will of the people. It implies that the people govern themselves through their chosen representatives. The government is elected through regular elections on the basis of universal adult franchise without any distinction or criteria like literacy, property, income, religion, caste, creed, sex etc. In fact, it's a government of the people, by the people and for the people.

Republic

The term 'Republic' implies a State in which people are supreme, and all public offices are open to every citizen without any distinction. There is no hereditary ruler. India is republic because the President, the Head of the State is elected by the elected members of Parliament and State Legislative Assemblies. His term of office is five years, and he runs his government through elected representatives of the people.

Justice, Liberty, Equality and Fraternity

The terms Sovereign, Socialist, Secular, Democratic and Republic denote the nature of Indian political system. But the Preamble also mentions the objectives of the constitution. They are Justice, Liberty, Equality and Fraternity. The Preamble seeks to secure to all its citizens without any discrimination social, economic and political justice; liberty of thought, expression, belief, faith and worship; equality of status and opportunity. It also wants fraternity among the citizens which must assure the dignity of the individual. In the minds of the founding fathers, the supreme objective was to improve the quality of life for the individual, to enable every citizen to live a life of dignity. The Indian society is highly heterogeneous, and widely segmented with diverse pulls and pressures. The terms 'Unity and Integrity of the Nation' were included in the Preamble later by the 42nd Amendment Act with the aim to build a united and integrated India.

5

KEY PARTS OF THE CONSTITUTION OF INDIA

Part I: The Union and its Territory

Part I of the Indian Constitution declares that India, i.e. Bharat, shall be Union of States. India has 28 States and 8 Union Territories as on March 31, 2024. Each State/UT of India has a unique demography, history and culture, dress, festivals, language etc. The Union Territories are administered by the Union Government. No State has a right to secede from the Union. It is indestructible union. The Parliament has the power to create new States or make suitable changes in the existing States. For instance, Chhattisgarh is a new state and was created under this provision by altering the boundaries of Madhya Pradesh.

Part II: Citizenship

A citizen is usually a permanent resident of a nation, and owes full allegiance to the State. He is entitled to its protection, and enjoys all the citizenship rights in the matter of employment, voting, holding of public office, etc.

Part II says that every person who has his domicile in India and was born in India, or whose parents or grandparents were born in India shall be the citizen of India. There are some provisions for persons who migrated from Pakistan, and Indians residing in foreign countries. It also lays down the procedure for becoming a citizen of India. All citizens have the same rights and duties all over the country without any discrimination.

Part III: Fundamental Rights

Fundamental Rights protect citizens against the arbitrary

and absolute exercise of power by the State. The section on Fundamental Rights has often been referred as the conscience of India Constitution. This part provides important civil and political rights to Indian citizens. They have been described in a very comprehensive and detailed manner. Some of them are available against the State but some of them are available against the individual also. They can be suspended in certain cases. Moreover, the Parliament can make amendments to them. Therefore, we say that they are not absolute in nature.

Indian Constitution guarantees following Fundamental Rights:

1. **Right to Equality (Article 14,15,16,17 & 18):** All citizens have been guaranteed that the State will not deny them equality before the law, or equal protection of law. No citizen can be discriminated on the basis of religion, race, caste, sex and place of birth or any of them. All citizens will have equal opportunities in matters of public employment but reservation may be made in favour of

scheduled castes, scheduled tribes and backward classes. The practice of untouchability has been abolished and the State cannot confer titles to citizens except for military and academic distinctions.

2. **Right to Freedom (Articles 19, 20, 21, 21-A & 22)**

The Right to freedom ensures personal and civil liberties to the people of India and, therefore, is regarded as the backbone of the Fundamental Rights. It protects the individual from the repressive and arbitrary acts of the government. Article 19 guarantees six types of rights to freedom:

(i) Right to freedom of speech and expression

(ii) Right to assemble peacefully and without arms

(iii) Right to form associations or unions

(iv) Right to move freely throughout the territory of India

(v) Right to reside and settle in any part of the territory of India, and

(vi) Right to practice any profession, or to carry on any occupation, trade or business

Article 20 and 22 provide for safeguards to a person who is accused of crime. Such a person can only be punished if proven guilty in a Court of law. A person arrested must be informed of the reasons of his arrest and he has to be produced before the nearest court of the magistrate within 24 hours, and he cannot be detained for more than the said period without the orders of the magistrate. Article 21 confers to every person the fundamental right to life and personal liberty. However, Article 21 has a wider meaning. It includes right to live with human dignity, freedom from exploitation, right to livelihood, right to speedy trial, right to clean water, right to freedom from noise pollution, right to clean environment etc. Article 21-A provides free and compulsory education to all children of the age six to fourteen years.

3. Right against Exploitation (Articles 23 & 24)

Trafficking of human beings, begging and other similar

forms of forced labour are prohibited. Bonded labour system has been abolished. Article 24 prohibits the employment of children below the age of fourteen years in hazardous enterprises, factories, mines or construction works.

4. **Right to Freedom of Religion (Articles 25, 26, 27 & 28)**

We are a secular country, and all the persons have a right to follow, practice and propagate their religion. The State cannot discriminate on the basis of religion; and followers of every religion have a right to manage their religious affairs.

5. **Cultural and Educational Rights (Articles 29 & 30)**

These are the rights given to minorities. All the minorities have a right to preserve their distinct language, script and culture. They also have the right to establish and administer their institutions.

6. Right to Constitutional Remedies (Article 32)

The Right to Constitutional Remedies has been called as the heart and soul of our Constitution. This article gives right to move Supreme Court or High Court in case the fundamental rights are violated. The Supreme Court or High Court issues orders or writs for the enforcement these fundamental rights.

The Fundamental Rights are not absolute. They have been subjected to certain restrictions but they should be reasonable. They can be suspended during emergency. They can also be amended by the Parliament.

Usually, acts are passed by a simple majority, i.e. more than half the votes cast. However, for a Constitutional amendment to be passed, you require two-thirds of the votes in both the Lok sabha and the Rajya Sabha.

The original Constitution incorporated Right to property also in the list of Fundamental Rights, but the same was eliminated from that list of Fundamental Rights by 44th Amendment in **1978**, and converted it into a legal right under Article 300 A.

The Supreme Court, in the famous Kesavananda Bharati case in 1973, had already restricted the amending power of the Parliament. The apex court had held that the Parliament could not amend the basic structure of the Constitution. This 'basic structure' doctrine has since been interpreted to include secularism, federalism, democracy, supremacy of the Constitution, rule of law, Independence of the judiciary, doctrine of separation of powers, parliamentary system of government, principle of free and fair elections, welfare state, etc. These features of the Constitution cannot be amended by the Parliament. In the past four decades, this decision has governed all interpretation of the Constitution.

Part IV: Directive Principles of State Policy

The framers of the Constitution knew that the ideals of

political justice would remain incomplete unless they were accompanied by the social and economic rights. It was their firm belief that the democracy could not be a success in a society where there were grave social and economic inequalities. But India was a poor country and could not provide social and economic rights to its people. Besides, there were other objectives which framers wanted the free India to achieve and, so, they wanted to mention them in the Constitution. Here the Irish Constitution came to their rescue where there was a chapter on Directive Principles of State Policy which could not be legally enforceable immediately but they were directives to the State to work in particular directions and the framers decided to have a similar chapter in the Indian Constitution.

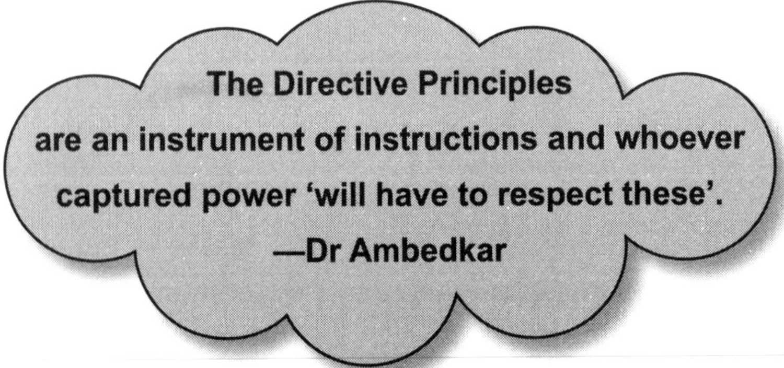

These Directive Principles cover different areas, but broadly, can be classified in three categories:

1. Directive Principles aimed at establishing a Welfare State in India. They are also termed as Socialist principles

2. Gandhian principles and

3. Liberal-Intellectual principles

    1. **Principles of Welfare State:** The principles of welfare state provides active obligation on the part of the State in removing inequalities in the country. Article 38 states, "The state shall strive to promote the welfare of the people by securing and protecting as effectively as it may be a social order in which justice, social, economic and political, shall form in all the institutions of the National life." The inequalities in income are to be minimised and inequalities in terms of status, facilities and opportunities are to be eliminated both at the level of individual as well as group. The State is to work in such a manner so that

all the citizens, men and women, equally have the right to an adequate means of livelihood and a decent standard of life. There should not be concentration of wealth; and men and women should get equal pay for equal work. The children are to be given opportunities to develop in a healthy manner, and are protected against exploitation. There should be right to work, right to education, and to public assistance in certain cases, and provisions for maternity relief, free legal aid to the poor, and workers participation in industry etc.

2. **Gandhian Principles:** Our father of the Nation, Mahatma Gandhi, while leading the freedom struggle had a vision of India which has been included in the Directive Principles of the State policy. The State should organise village panchayats and provide them with adequate powers. It should also prohibit the slaughter of cow and other animals which are yielding milk. The promotion of educational and economic interests of the weaker sections,

in particular, of Scheduled Castes and Scheduled Tribes; and prohibition of intoxicating drinks and drugs etc. are the directives given to the State which were dear to Mahatma Gandhi.

3. **Liberal Intellectual Principles:** These principles aim to create a society based on equality and individual liberty. In our society, there have been different sets of rules governing personal matters like marriage, adoption, divorce, and maintenance for different communities. Therefore, it becomes difficult for people to know which law applies to them. There is a lot of social inequality and gender injustice in many religions in India. Therefore Article 44 of the Constitution says "The State shall endeavour to secure for the citizens a uniform civil code throughout the territory of India." There are other liberal intellect directives like separation of the judiciary from the executive, conservation of monuments, etc. There are also directives to the State in international area. Article 51 declares that

the State shall endeavour to (a) promote international peace and security; (b) maintain just and honourable relations between nations; and (c) the settlement of international disputes by arbitration.

Many of the Directive Principles have been criticised for being moral precepts or vague. The State cannot be compelled to enforce them. But, certainly they lay down a foundation of a welfare state, and they are the yardsticks of success of a particular government. In fact, after the implementation of the Constitution many of them have been enforced also.

A Directive under Article 45 to provide free and compulsory education to children until the age of fourteen years has been made a fundamental right under Article 21A.

Part IV-A: Fundamental Duties

This part deals with the fundamental duties of the citizens of India. It is always believed that whenever there are rights to be enjoyed, there are certain responsibilities attached to it. These are called the Fundamental Duties, which every citizen should follow.

In 1976, the 42nd Amendment of the Constitution was passed. Among other things, the amendment inserted a list of Fundamental Duties of the citizens. In all ten duties were enumerated. However constitution does not say any thing about enforcing these Duties. These Fundamental Duties have an educative value and they visualised the basics of a responsible citizenship. Constitution does not make the enjoyment of rights dependent or conditional upon fulfillment of duties, Supreme Court has ruled that the Fundamental Duties are binding on citizens.

Following are the fundamental Duties:

1. To abide by the Indian Constitution and respect its ideals and institutions, the National Flag and the National Anthem;

2. To cherish and follow the noble ideals that inspired the national struggle for freedom;

3. To uphold and protect the sovereignty, unity and integrity of India;

4. To defend the country and render national service when called upon to do so;

5. To promote harmony and the spirit of common brotherhood amongst all the people of India transcending religious, linguistic and regional or sectional diversities and to renounce practices derogatory to the dignity of women;

6. To value and preserve the rich heritage of our composite culture;

7. To protect and improve the natural environment including forests, lakes, rivers and wildlife, and to have compassion for living creatures;

8. To develop scientific temper, humanism and the spirit of inquiry and reform;

9. To safeguard public property and to abjure violence;

10. To strive towards excellence in all spheres of individual and collective activity so that the nation constantly rises to higher levels of endeavour and achievement;

11. To provide opportunities for education to every child or ward between the age of six and fourteen years. This duty was added by the 86th Constitutional Amendment Act, 2002.

Parties and politicians who use religion, casteism, separatism, etc. for capturing power are clearly violating their Fundamental Duties under the Constitution.

It is the duty of every citizen to ensure that our monuments are not damaged, disfigured, subjected to vandalism or greed of unscrupulous people.

Like the directive principles of State Policy, the inclusion of fundamental duties has been criticised. They cannot be enforced in a court of law and are moral precepts, and therefore, have no place in the Constitution. But they remind and educate the citizens of India regarding their duties to the nation and the society.

Supreme Court has said that the basis of composite culture of our country is Sanskrit language and its literature; therefore Sanskrit language should be included in our education system (A.I.R. 1994 S.C. 1918 & 1994-6 S.C.C. 579). Article 351 says it shall be the duty of the Union to promote the spread of the Hindi language with the help of Sanskrit Vocabulary wherever necessary.

Part V: The Union and Part VI: The States

Part V and VI of the Indian Constitution deals with the political and judicial structure of our country. India is a federal country and therefore, we have Union and the States' governments. The structures of Union Government and State Government have been given in Part IV and Part V respectively. We have also adopted parliamentary form of government at both the levels. At the Union level, we have President as the head of the State who is actually a ceremonial head. The Head of the Government is the Prime Minister who along with his Council of Ministers is collectively responsible to the Lok Sabha (House of the People), Parliament of India.

All executive power of the Union is vested in the President, yet his position is conceived as that of a constitutional head of the State.

The Parliament is the Union legislature which has two Houses - Lok Sabha, the Lower House or popular House which is elected directly by the people of India, and Rajya Sabha, the Upper House which has representatives of the States of India, and is constituted on the basis of indirect elections.

The two Houses of Parliament enjoy co-equal power and status in all spheres except in financial matters.

Any Indian citizen can contest the election to the Parliament, and for Lok Sabha, he should be at least 25 years of age, and in case of Rajya Sabha, his minimum age should be 30 years. We have Universal Adult Franchise, which means that all the citizens of India, of the age of 18 and above, are eligible to vote without any distinction of caste, creed, religion, sex or other considerations. While the Parliament is the legislative organ of the government responsible to make the laws, the executive comprises of Prime Minister and his Council of Ministers.

The function of Parliament is to exercise political and financial control over the Executive and to ensure parliamentary surveillance of the administration.

Similar structure exists in States also. We have Governor as the head of the State, while the Chief Minister is the head of the government who along with his Council of Ministers is collectively responsible to State Legislative Assembly. In few states, we have two houses of legislature, Legislative Assembly and Legislative Council, in which the Legislative Assembly is directly elected by the people of the State while the members of Legislative Council are elected indirectly. Most of the legislatures of the States have only legislative assembly. **The Governor can dissolve the Legislative Assembly of the State. Without his assent, no Bill can become law even after it has been passed by the two Houses.**

The legislature makes laws and the executive implements them. Then, there is a third organ of the government which is Judiciary. The job of the Judiciary is to see that the constitution and the laws are obeyed. It has the power to punish those who violate the law or Constitution. There is one single unified judicial system. The judicial institutions in our country go up like a pyramid. At the lower level there are courts in the districts; there are high courts at the state level (Article 214) and on top of the pyramid at the apex level, we have one single Supreme Court (Article 124) for the entire country who is the guardian of the Constitution. In some cases a High Court has jurisdiction over more than one state and union territory (Article 231). Punjab and Haryana share a common High Court at Chandigarh, and the seven northeast states have a common High Court at Gowahati. Some High Courts have benches in other parts of the state for greater accessibility. The decisions made by the Supreme Court are binding on all other courts in India. The Supreme Court has original jurisdiction and appellate jurisdiction. The disputes between the Union and the States can be directly taken to Supreme Court for redressal.

There is no appeal against the judgement of the Supreme Court. It remains the law of the land unless its interpretation is reviewed or reversed by the Supreme Court itself or the law or the Constitution is suitably amended by Parliament.

In a case of violation of Fundamental Rights, the case can also be directly taken to the Supreme Court. This constitutes the original jurisdiction. It also has advisory jurisdiction which means that the President may consult the

Supreme Court on certain question of law or fact. The High Courts also have original jurisdiction regarding Fundamental Rights. The structure and functions of the subordinate district courts are similar. The decisions of the lower courts can be challenged in the High Courts. Each State has been divided into a number of districts and each of them is under a District Judge.

The Parliament in India is not as supreme as the British Parliament where no judicial review of legislation is permitted. At the same time our judiciary is not as supreme as in the USA which recognises no limit on the scope of judicial review.

Sometimes, the legislative or the executive organ of the government does not perform its duties. In such cases, the Courts step in and fill the gap. For example, there were numerous complaints of women being harassed in the workplaces but nothing concrete was done either by the executive or the legislative branch of the government. In 1997 Vishakha case, the Supreme Court laid down the guidelines and norms to prevent and punish the sexual harassment of women in workplaces; and those guidelines became law. Later on in 2013, the Parliament enacted the Sexual Harassment of Women at Workplace (Prevention, Prohibition and Redressal Act) The Supreme Court and other courts in India have been very active as the guardian of the Constitution. As the guardian of the Constitution, the court has to see that the law and the constitution are implemented, and justice is assured to each and every citizen of the country.

An independent and impartial judiciary is an essential requisite for ensuring human rights and protecting democracy.

Parts VII &VIII

Part VII was repealed by the Constitution (Seventh Amendment) Act, 1956. Part VIII deals with the administration of Union territories, and special provisions with respect to National Capital Region of Delhi. The Union territories are administered by the President through an administrator, and they do not have same constitutional status as States.

Part IX The Panchayats and the Municipalities

The Part V and VI provide for democratic set up at the Union and the State level. However, the democracy at the higher level can be a success only when you have democratic participation at the local level. This was an unfinished task in 1950 when the constitution was put into practice. This unfinished task was given due consideration in 1992 when 73rdand 74th amendments were made in the Constitution. The 73rd Constitutional Amendment gave constitutional status to the Panchayati Raj in the rural areas, and 74th Constitutional

Amendment mandated local self-government for the urban population. As per the 73rd amendment, three tier Panchayati Raj system --- village Panchayat, Panchayat Samities and District Panchayat --- have been established in most of the States, and they have been assigned enough functions and powers to enable them to function as effective institutions of self-government. The representatives in all the three tiers are elected by the people. They have also been assigned sources of revenues so that they are able to function effectively. Similarly, the 74th Constitutional Amendment provides for local self government in urban areas. Here, three types of municipalities have been provided --- Nagar Panchayat, Municipal Council and Municipal Corporation. All the seats in these municipalities are also elected and further provisions have been madc to involvc thc local population through Wards Committees. **Can you believe that in the Panchayati Raj institutions alone at the rural level, we have more than three million representatives directly elected by the people? No other country in the world has so many elected representatives.**

It was hoped that the new Panchayats and Municipalities would begin a new era of real representative and participatory democracy with nearly three and a half million elected representatives—one third of them women, involved in the business of governance all over India thereby bringing power to the people where it belongs.

Part X: The Scheduled and Tribal Areas

Part X deals with the administration of Scheduled Areas and Tribal Areas in north-eastern part of the country.

Part XI: Relations between the Union and the States

Parliament makes laws for the whole or any part of the country, while the Legislature of a State make laws for the whole or part of the State. The Seventh Schedule has been added to the Constitution which contains the division of power between the Union and the States. For this purpose, three lists have been made. The Parliament has exclusive power to make laws in the items enumerated in the List I, the Union List. List II, the State List contains items in which the State has the power to make laws, and there is List III, the Concurrent List containing matters in which both the Union as well as the States can make laws. Matters not mentioned in any list are the subject matters of the Parliament. This is also called the Residuary Power of legislation. Since, we have a strong Union government, in many cases the Parliament has the power to legislate on the subjects mentioned in the State List. During Emergency, the Parliament gets the power to make law on any matter enumerated in the State List. Similarly, though the States have executive power yet the Union Government has, under different situations, many administrative powers to exercise control over the States. This has been done to ensure unity and integrity of our country.

Imposition of President's rule over the States by the Union, has been one of the most criticised and controversial provision of the Constitution.

Part XV: Elections

Elections are life and blood of a democracy, and without free and fair elections no democracy can work. For this purpose, the Election Commission is vested with the power of superintendence, direction and control of the preparation of electoral rolls, and conduct of all the elections to the Parliament and Legislature of every State, and to the offices of President and Vice-President. It has also been made clear that there shall be no discrimination based on religion, race, caste or sex in electoral matters. Elections in India have been conducted in a very free and fair manner, and we constitute one of the most stable democracies in the world.

Part XVI: Reservation

The Constitution of India empowers the State for making special provisions for the advancement of any socially and educationally backward classes of citizens of the Scheduled Castes and the Scheduled Tribes. One of the Directive Principles of the State Policy also states that "The State shall promote with special care the educational and economic interests of the weaker sections of the people, and, in particular, of the Scheduled Castes and the Scheduled Tribes, and shall protect them from social injustice and all forms of exploitation." The Scheduled Castes and Scheduled Tribes have been provided with 15 percent and 7.5 percent reservation in public sector and government-aided educational institutes. Besides, 27 percent reservation is for the benefit of Other Backward Classes (OBCs), and further 10 percent reservation has been made for the economically weaker section of the General category. However, the Supreme Court has ruled that the reservation should not exceed 50 per cent.

Part XVII: Official Language

Article 343 says that the official language of the Union shall be Hindi in Devnagari script. The form of numerals to be used for the official purposes of the Union shall be the international form of the Indian numerals. But, the English language also continues to be used as official language along with Hindi. However, the States can have their own official language. The Eighth Schedule of the Constitution enumerates 22 regional languages including Sanskrit and Urdu. But the Constitution also makes it clear (A-348) that all proceedings in the Supreme Court and High Courts, the Bills and Acts passed by the Parliament or State legislatures, all the Ordinances, Notifications issued by the President or Governor shall be in English language.

Part XVIII: Emergency Provisions

When the Constitution was being framed, there were many dangers to the unity, stability and security of our country from internal and external forces. A few were even predicting that India may not remain one and will break down. Therefore, the framers decided to have Emergency provisions in the Constitution to enable the Union Government to safeguard the unity and integrity of the country. The Constitution provides for three kinds of Emergency – 1) National Emergency (A-352) which is imposed when there is a threat to the security of the country due to external aggression or war or by an armed conflict; 2) Emergency in case of failure of constitutional machinery in the States (A-356) (in popular language it is called President's Rule; 3) Financial Emergency (A-360) when the financial stability or credit of the country is threatened. All the three Emergencies are proclaimed in different situations and have different impacts.

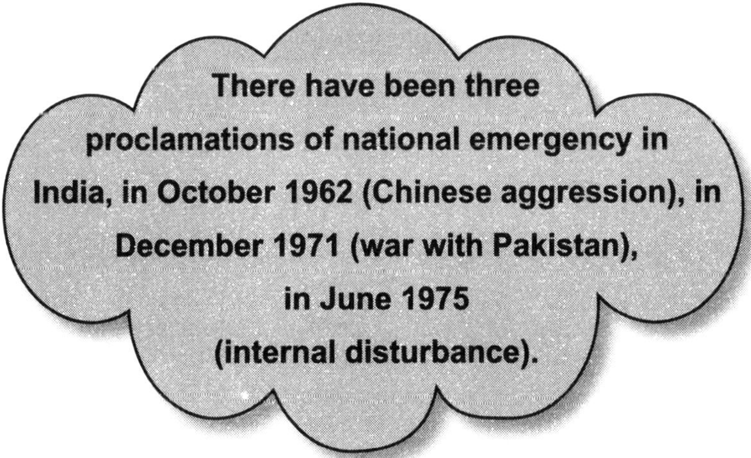

Part XX: Amendment of the Constitution

A Constitution is a dynamic document and it should grow with the passage of time. It has to change with the changing time. Therefore, every constitution has a provision of amending it. The Indian Constitution has also adapted itself to the changing time. This Part deals with the Procedure of Amending the Constitution, and as on August 2021, it has been amended 106 times since the Constitution was implemented in 1950. The Supreme Court of India has made it clear that the Basic Structure of the Constitution cannot be amended. The 106th amendment, known as Nari Shakti Vandan Act, 2023, reserves one third of all seats for women in Lok Sabha, State legislative Assemblies, and the Legislative Assembly of the National Capital Territory of Delhi for 15 years.

This reservation is expected to significantly enhance the nation's development, particularly for women, by tackling the underlying socioeconomic and political disparities.

Parliament can in any way amend, alter or repeal any provision of the Constitution and such amendments cannot be questioned in any court of law on any ground whatsoever unless they tend to alter or violate what may be considered as the basic features of the Constitution by the Supreme Court.

Conclusion: The framers of our Constitution fixed the rules of governance for the generations to come. It was also felt that this constitution would remove poverty and other socio-economic problems in our country. They wanted our country to become a prosperous and colourful democracy. We are heading toward our ideals and goals. Our country has changed a lot thanks to our constitution and a day will come when the ideals and goals of the Constitution will become a reality.

■■■